bake me I'm yours...
cupcake celebration

Lindy Smith

D&C

David and Charles

www.rucraft.co.uk

A DAVID & CHARLES BOOK

Copyright © David & Charles Limited 2010

David & Charles is an F+W Media Inc. company
4700 East Galbraith Road, Cincinnati,
OH 45236

First published in the UK and US in 2010
Reprinted in 2010, 2011, 2012

Text and designs copyright © Lindy Smith 2010
Layout and photography copyright © David &
Charles 2010

Lindy Smith has asserted her right to be
identified as author of this work in accordance
with the Copyright, Designs and Patents
Act, 1988.

Names of manufacturers and products are
provided for the information of readers, with
no intention to infringe copyright or trademarks.

A catalogue record for this book is available
from the British Library.

ISBN-13: 978-0-7153-3770-7 hardback
ISBN-10: 0-7153-3770-X hardback

Printed in China by Toppan Leefung
Printing Limited
for David & Charles
Brunel House   Newton Abbot   Devon

Acquisitions Editor Jennifer Fox-Proverbs
Assistant Editor Jeni Hennah
Project Editor Emily Pitcher
Design Manager Sarah Clark
Art Editor Charly Bailey
Designer Dawn Taylor
Photographer Sian Irvine
Production Controller Kelly Smith
Pre-Press Jodie Culpin and Natasha Jorden

David and Charles publish high quality books
on a wide range of subjects. For more great
book ideas visit: **www.rucraft.co.uk**

contents

introduction...

Cupcakes are taking the world by storm, and I think I know why – put simply, baking and decorating cupcakes is fun, rewarding and not too time consuming. On my travels around the globe I've seen cupcakes in all shapes and sizes, in tiny little boutique cake shops and large supermarkets. I have also been given them as welcome gifts – everyone loves a cupcake!

I'm completely hooked on making cupcakes, and you probably will be too after reading this book! I've included some fabulously tasty recipes that are easy and straightforward to make, and I hope you enjoy experimenting with them as much as I have! Most cupcake recipes only take 20 minutes to bake, so by the time you've washed up and put everything away the cakes are ready – now that's what I call perfect timing.

Cupcake decorating is all about personal taste, imagination and suitability for the occasion. There are endless possibilities, so I hope that the cupcakes I have created on the following pages will inspire you to have a go or to be a little bit more adventurous. I have used different types of coverings to appeal to all palettes, and have really pushed the boat out when it comes to the actual decoration.

I want to put the humble cupcake at centre stage to show the world just what it can be – a beautiful, 'collectable', miniature work of art that is a true taste sensation and not just a fashionable cake to bake!

Have fun

Lindy

www.lindyscakes.co.uk

basic tools and equipment

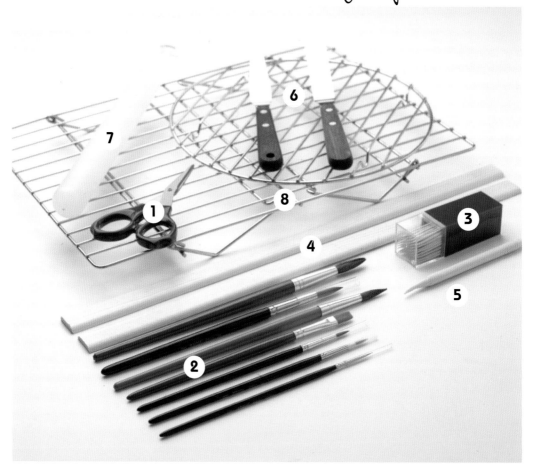

Before you begin it's a good idea to check that you have all of the right tools for the cakes you plan to bake and decorate. Included here is the equipment that you will need in your basic tool kit to make and decorate any cupcake. The more specific tools used in each project are included in the 'you will need' section at the start of each project.

1. Scissors: these are useful around the kitchen in general, but you will occasionally also need them for cutting modelling paste.

2. Paintbrushes: a range of sizes and weights for painting and dusting.

3. Cocktail sticks: handy for those little details, such as eyes.

4. Spacers: roll your paste out between them to ensure an even thickness.

5. Dresden tool: to create markings on paste.

6. Palette knife: vital for lifting and cutting sugarpaste.

7. Rolling pin: for rolling out different pastes. Non-stick are ideal.

8. Wire cooling rack: to rest your cupcakes while they cool before decorating.

baking equipment

Cupcake pans and cupcake cases are obviously essential requirements before you begin. It is important that the cases fit snugly inside the pans to ensure that they are supported while baking, otherwise your cakes will lose their shape and end up flattened.

pans

There are a range of sizes and shapes available. When choosing your pans select the size that you would like to bake, and then look at the shape of the cup – some have almost vertical sides, while others are much more angled. The difference, although not that visible when looking at a pan, makes a huge difference when decorating a cupcake – generally, the more angled the sides of the pan the more surface you have to decorate, while the more vertical sides leave you with less decorating area.

In this book I have used two different standard-sized cupcake (muffin) pans, and two different mini cupcake muffin pans.

cases

When choosing your cases it's important to consider the quality of the cupcake and the effect you are wanting to achieve. Cupcake cases are simply circles of paper, or foil-covered paper, that have been fluted to form a cup.

If you use thin cupcake cases (the type that you find in most supermarkets) you'll find that the cases turn translucent when baked. This can be used to good effect, but it is frustrating if you are using a patterned case and you want the design to be clearly visible. One way around this is to use a double or triple layer of cases. Alternatively, spend a little more money and buy foil-covered cases, or cases that are made from thicker, higher quality paper. Re-usable silicone cupcakes are also available in various colours.

Size is another factor to consider when choosing your cases – it is very much personal choice, but it does affect the amount of cake batter that you will require. The chart opposite will help you to estimate the number of cupcakes you can bake from the recipes in this book using various case sizes.

cupcake quantities

The number of cupcakes you can bake from a given recipe varies according to how much you fill your cases. If you want your cakes to rise above the cases you will naturally use more of the mixture than if you prefer the cakes to stay below the case tops.

	type	size		approximate quantities per cake recipe group*				
				1	2	3	4	5
mini	paper mini	67mm: Ht 20mm Base 27mm	(2⅝in) (¾in) (1in)	60	64	72	120	144
mini	foil mini	70mm: Ht 20mm Base 30mm	(2¾in) (¾in) (1³⁄₁₆in)	45	48	54	90	108
standard	UK small fairy cake	96mm: Ht 27mm Base 42mm	(3¾in) (1in) (1¾in)	26	27	31	51	62
standard	UK cupcake	105mm: Ht 30mm Base 45mm	(4⅛in) (1³⁄₁₆in) (1¾in)	20	21	24	40	48
standard	US cupcake	113mm: Ht 30mm Base 53mm	(4⅜in) (1³⁄₁₆in) (2⅛in)	18	19	22	36	43
standard	Swedish cupcake	116mm: Ht 33mm Base 50mm	(4⅝in) (1¼in) (2in)	16	17	20	33	39
standard	Australian cupcake	119mm: Ht 35mm Base 49mm	(4¾in) (1⅜in) (1⅞in)	15	16	18	30	36
muffin	UK muffin	120mm: Ht 37mm Base 46mm	(4¾in) (1½in) (1¾in)	12	13	14	24	29
muffin	US muffin	154mm: Ht 46mm Base 62mm	(6in) (1¾in) (2⅜in)	6	7	8	13	15

*cake recipe groups:
1 – ginger, pear and chocolate chip, lemon polenta
2 – orange and poppy seed
3 – honey
4 – chocolate and cherry mud cake, date and walnut
5 – hummingbird cake

please note: these figures are approximate and are intended as a guide

cupcake recipes

Cupcakes should be fun! First of all choose your cases (see p. 8 for guidance on types) and then choose a recipe to use. The recipes in this book are there to help and inspire you, but most cake recipes will work so please don't be afraid to experiment with flavours to create something unique to you.

tips for successful cupcake baking

- always use only the finest ingredients
- accurately measuring your ingredients is vital to cupcake success
- bring all your ingredients to room temperature before mixing your cupcake batter
- ensure your cupcake pan is thoroughly clean before adding the cases
- fill your cases by pouring or piping if the batter is thin or by using a spoon if it is thick
- preheat your oven and bake your cupcakes at the correct temperature. Oven thermometers are a useful check
- if your know your oven heat is uneven, rotate your pan halfway through the baking time
- using a fan oven can dry out small cakes quickly, so reduce the temperature stated in each recipe by 10 degrees

- cupcakes must be completely cold before decorating
- undecorated cupcakes can usually be frozen for up to a month

If you decide to experiment with other recipes here are some points to bear in mind:

- each cake recipe will rise differently; some recipes don't rise at all while some others double in size, so I suggest you make a trial batch filling the cupcakes at different levels in the cases to find the optimum height for your recipe
- typically cupcakes bake for around 20 minutes, but ovens vary so test and retest as necessary
- make a note of the shape of the top of the cupcake; some will be fairly flat whilst others will be quite domed. The shape can be important when choosing the type of decoration you wish to use

sticky ginger

If you want a moist, sticky cake this fits the bill perfectly. These cupcakes are best eaten within a week.

you will need

- 120g/4¼oz unsalted butter
- 100g/3½oz soft dark brown sugar (molasses sugar)
- 4 tbsp/60ml golden syrup (corn syrup)
- 4 tbsp/60ml black treacle (molasses)
- 150ml/¼ pint milk
- 2 large eggs, beaten
- 1½tsp/7.5ml vanilla extract
- 4 pieces of stem ginger, drained from syrup and chopped
- 230g/8oz self-raising flour
- 25g/1oz ground ginger
- 1 tsp/5ml mixed spice

1 Preheat oven to 170°C/325°F/Gas 3.

2 Line the trays with cupcake cases.

3 Place butter, sugar, golden syrup and black treacle into a pan and warm over a low heat until the sugar has dissolved.

4 Stir in the milk and allow the mixture to cool slightly – you need to make sure that it is not so hot that the eggs cook when they go in it. If you are in a hurry you can stand the saucepan in cold water so that it cools more quickly.

5 Beat in the eggs, vanilla and stem ginger.

6 Sift flour and spices into a bowl and make a well in the centre. Gradually pour the liquid into the well and beat with a wooden spoon until combined.

7 Pour or pipe the mixture into the cupcake cases – they should be about three quarters full.

8 Bake for about 20 minutes, or until a fine skewer inserted into the centre of one of the cupcakes comes out clean.

9 Allow the cupcakes to cool in the pan for 5 minutes, before removing them to a wire rack to cool completely.

orange and poppy seed

The tangy flavour and interesting texture of the poppy seeds and orange peel are a winning combination, and are bound to have you hooked! This recipe would also work well substituting the orange for lemon. Best eaten within two weeks.

you will need

- 185g/6½oz unsalted butter
- 160g/5½oz caster sugar
- 100g/3½oz marmalade
- ¼tsp/1ml almond extract
- zest of two oranges
- 80ml/3fl oz orange juice
- 185g/6½oz self-raising flour
- 60g/2oz ground almonds
- 40g/1½oz poppy seeds
- 50g/2oz mixed peel
- 3 large eggs, lightly beaten

1 Preheat oven to 170°C/325°F/Gas 3.

2 Line the trays with cupcake cases.

3 Place butter, sugar, marmalade, almond extract, orange zest and juice in a pan and stir over low heat until the mixture is melted. Allow to cool.

4 Sift flour, almonds and poppy seeds into a bowl, add the mixed peel, then make a well in the centre.

5 Gradually pour the cooled liquid into the well and mix until smooth.

6 Add the eggs and mix until combined.

7 Pour or pipe the mixture into the cupcake cases until they are about three quarters full.

8 Bake for 20 minutes, or until a fine skewer inserted into the centre of one of the cakes comes out clean.

9 Allow to cool in the pan for 5 minutes before removing them to a wire rack to cool completely.

10 Brush with an orange liquor, such as Cointreau or Grand Marnier, before decorating.

hummingbird

This recipe originates from the southern states of America and is a moist, delicious cake that works beautifully as a cupcake, but is best eaten within 3 days of baking. If you like carrot cake then you'll love this too!

you will need

- ♡ 250g/9oz plain flour
- ♡ 125g/4½oz self-raising flour
- ♡ 1 tsp/5ml bicarbonate of soda (baking soda)
- ♡ 1 tsp/5ml cinnamon
- ♡ 2 x 450g/16oz tins crushed pineapple in juice
- ♡ 400g/14oz soft brown sugar
- ♡ 80g/3oz dessicated coconut
- ♡ 400g/14oz (about 4) ripe bananas, mashed
- ♡ 4 large eggs, lightly beaten
- ♡ 325ml/10½fl oz vegetable oil
- ♡ 2tsp/10ml vanilla extract
- ♡ 120g/4oz pecans, chopped (traditional but optional)

1 Preheat oven to 170°C/325°F/Gas 3.

2 Line the trays with cupcake cases.

3 In a large bowl, sift together flours, bicarb, sugar and cinnamon.

4 Drain the pineapple and reserve 125ml/4fl oz of juice.

5 Add the remaining ingredients to the bowl, including the reserved juice, and mix until combined.

6 Pour or pipe the mixture into the cupcake cases until they are about three quarters full.

7 Bake for about 20 minutes, or until a fine skewer inserted into the centre of one of the cupcakes comes out clean.

8 Allow to cool in the tray for 5 minutes before removing them to a wire rack to cool completely.

chocolate cherry mud

If you've never tried a mud cake, treat yourself to this one! Mud cakes are very rich, sweet, dense in texture and utterly divine. The subtle addition of cherry brandy makes this one for adults only! Best eaten within two weeks.

you will need

- ♡ 425g/15oz tin stoneless black cherries in syrup
- ♡ 330g/11½oz unsalted butter
- ♡ 200g/7oz dark chocolate
- ♡ 600g/21oz caster sugar
- ♡ 120ml/4fl oz cherry brandy
- ♡ 300g/10½oz plain flour, sifted
- ♡ 75g/3oz self-raising flour, sifted
- ♡ 75g/3oz cocoa powder, sifted
- ♡ 3 large eggs

1 Preheat oven to 160°C/320°F/Gas 3.

2 Line the trays with cupcake cases.

3 Drain the cherries, reserving the syrup. Add water to syrup to make 250ml/9fl oz of liquid. Process or finely chop the cherries.

4 Place the cherries, syrup, butter, chocolate, sugar and brandy into a pan, and warm over a low heat until the chocolate and butter have melted. Allow mixture to cool to room temperature – you don't want the eggs to start cooking when they go in the mixture.

5 Whisk in the flours, cocoa and then the eggs.

6 Pour or pipe the mixture into the cupcake cases until they are about three quarters full.

7 Bake for about 45 minutes, or until a fine skewer inserted into the centre of one of the cupcakes comes out clean.

8 Allow the cupcakes to cool in the pan 5 minutes before removing them to a wire rack to cool completely.

date and walnut

This low fat old-fashioned favourite has a lovely light but moist texture. It's delightfully easy to make, and keeps well too. Eat within two weeks.

you will need

- 250ml/9fl oz golden syrup
- 60g/2¼oz unsalted butter
- 250ml/9fl oz milk
- 300g/10½oz wholemeal flour
- 300g/10½oz plain flour
- 220g/7¾oz soft brown sugar
- 1 tbsp/15ml baking powder
- 1 tsp/5ml baking soda
- 200g/7oz walnuts, chopped
- 500g/17½oz pitted dates, chopped
- 1 large egg, beaten

1 Preheat oven to 180°C/350°F/Gas 4.

2 Line the trays with cupcake cases.

3 Place golden syrup, butter and milk in a saucepan and stir over low heat until the mixture is melted and smooth. Do not boil. Allow to cool slightly.

4 Place the flours, sugar, baking powder, baking soda, walnuts and dates together in a large bowl.

5 Combine the melted and dry ingredients and mix well. Add the egg and mix.

6 Spoon or pipe the thick mixture into the cupcake cases until they are about two thirds full.

7 Bake for about 20–25 minutes, or until a fine skewer inserted into the centre of one cupcake comes out clean.

8 Allow to cool in the tray for 5 minutes before removing to a wire rack to cool completely.

pear and chocolate chip

What a wonderful combination – you'll have to try it for yourself to find out just how sublime it is! If pears are not in season then try substituting with apples. Best eaten within four days.

you will need

- ♡ 175g/6oz unsalted butter
- ♡ 140g/5oz soft light brown sugar
- ♡ 140g/5oz self-raising flour
- ♡ 100g/3½oz ground almonds
- ♡ 2 large eggs, beaten
- ♡ 5 ripe conference pears
- ♡ 100g/3½oz dark chocolate chips or chocolate cut into chunks

1 Preheat oven to 160°C/320°F/Gas 3.

2 Line the trays with cupcake cases.

3 Place the butter and sugar into a pan and warm over a low heat until the butter has melted. Allow mixture to cool slightly.

4 Sift flour and ground almonds into a bowl and make a well in the centre.

5 When the melted mixture has cooled beat in the eggs, then gradually pour the cooled liquid into the well of the dry ingredients and mix until smooth.

6 Peel, core and finely chop the pears, then stir into the batter together with the chocolate.

7 Spoon the mixture into the baking cases. They should be about three quarters full.

8 Bake for about 20 minutes, or until a fine skewer inserted into the centre of one of the cupcakes comes out clean.

9 Allow to cool in the tray for 5 minutes before removing to a wire rack to cool completely.

lemon polenta

This delicious lemon cake is unusual but excitingly tangy with a wonderful texture. This recipe works well with gluten-free flour. Best eaten within four days.

you will need

- 3 large eggs
- 200g/7oz caster sugar
- 5tbsp/75ml natural yoghurt
- 5tbsp/75ml sunflower oil
- grated zest and juice of two lemons
- 175g/6oz polenta
- 50g/2oz plain flour or gluten-free flour
- 1½tsp/7.5ml baking powder

1 Preheat oven to 170°C/325°F/Gas 3.

2 Line the trays with cupcake cases.

3 In a mixing bowl, beat the eggs and sugar until pale and creamy.

4 In a separate bowl, stir in the yoghurt, oil, lemon rind and 2 tablespoons (30ml) of lemon juice (reserve the remaining lemon juice for the syrup) until combined.

5 Add the yoghurt mixture into the eggs and sugar, beating continuously with a wooden spoon until smooth.

6 Sift the polenta, flour and baking powder into the batter

7 Using a jug, pour the mixture (which is fairly runny) into the paper cases. They should be about three quarters full.

8 Bake for 20 minutes, or until a skewer inserted into the centre of one of the cupcakes comes out clean.

9 Allow to cool in the tray for 5 minutes before removing to a wire rack.

10 Prick the top of the cupcakes and pour a little of the syrup over each.

lemon syrup

Place 3tbsp/45ml of caster sugar, the reserved lemon juice and 2tbsp/30ml of water into a pan. Dissolve the sugar on a low heat, then boil for a couple of minutes. Use when warm.

honey cake

A beautifully simple cake, with the flavour very much determined by the honey that you use. Best eaten within a week.

you will need

- 225g/8oz unsalted butter
- 250g/9oz clear honey (the better the quality, the better the flavour!)
- 100g/4oz soft light brown sugar
- 3 large eggs, beaten
- 300g/10oz self-raising flour, sifted

1 Preheat oven to 160°C/320°F/Gas 3.

2 Line bun or muffin trays with paper cupcake cases.

3 Place the butter, honey and sugar into a saucepan and warm over a low heat until the sugar has dissolved and the butter melted. Boil the mixture for one minute, then allow to cool and thicken.

4 Beat the eggs into the cooled mixture.

5 Place the flour into a bowl, then beat in the honey mixture until you have a smooth batter.

6 Spoon or pour the mixture into the baking cases so that they are about two thirds full.

7 Bake for about 25 minutes, or until a fine skewer inserted into the centre of one of the cupcakes comes out clean.

8 Allow to cool in the tray for 5 minutes before removing them to a wire rack.

9 Warm 2tbsps/30ml of honey in a small pan and brush over the tops of the cakes to glaze. Allow to cool completely.

decoration recipes

There is a huge choice when it comes to adding a frosting or topping to your cupcake. Here are some recipes for my favourites, but don't be afraid to try others or adapt and flavour the ones below.

standard buttercream

you will need

- ♡ 110g/3¾oz unsalted (sweet) butter
- ♡ 350g/12oz icing (confectioners') sugar
- ♡ 15–30ml/1–2 tbsp milk or water
- ♡ a few drops of vanilla extract or flavouring of your choice

A popular choice for cupcakes. Although traditional buttercream doesn't have the same versatility as some of the other covering materials, it will still struggle to be beaten when it's done well.

1 Place the butter in a bowl and beat until light and fluffy.

2 Sift the icing sugar into the bowl and continue to beat until the mixture changes colour.

3 Add just enough milk or water to give a firm but spreadable consistency.

4 Flavour by adding the vanilla or alternative flavouring, then store the buttercream in an airtight container in a refrigerator until required. Re-beat before using.

> flavouring buttercream
> Try replacing the liquid in the recipe with:
> ♡ alcohols, such as whisky or brandy
> ♡ other liquids, such as coffee, melted chocolate, lemon curd or fresh fruit purees
> Or add:
> ♡ nut butters to make a praline flavour
> ♡ flavourings, such as mint or rose extract

swiss meringue buttercream

This buttercream is less sweet than the standard buttercream, and has a beautiful glossy finish that doesn't fade. This buttercream is not stable above 15°C/ 59°F, however, so is not suitable for hot days or climates!

you will need

- ♥ 4 large egg whites
- ♥ 250g/9oz caster sugar
- ♥ 250g/9oz unsalted butter, softened
- ♥ a few drops of vanilla extract

1 Place the egg whites and sugar into a bowl over a pan of simmering water. Stir while heating to prevent the egg whites cooking.

2 Once the sugar crystals have dissolved, remove the bowl from the heat and whisk the meringue to its full volume and the mixture is cool – about 5 minutes.

3 Add the butter and vanilla and continue to whisk for about 10 minutes – the mixture will reduce in volume and look curdled, but don't panic! Keep whisking until the icing has a smooth, light and fluffy texture.

4 Store in a refrigerator for up to two days, and re-beat before using.

colouring buttercream
Add liquid or paste food colouring a little at a time into the icing and beat between each addition until you achieve the colour required.

chocolate ganache

A must for all chocoholics – use the best dark chocolate you can source for a really indulgent topping.

dark chocolate ganache:

- ♡ 200g/7oz dark chocolate
- ♡ 200ml/7fl oz cream

white chocolate:

- ♡ 600g/1lb 5oz white chocolate
- ♡ 80ml/2¾fl oz cream

1 Melt the chocolate and cream together in a bowl over a saucepan of gently simmering water, stirring occasionally to combine. Alternatively, use a microwave on low power, stirring thoroughly every 20 seconds or so. Be careful, however, as the chocolate can burn quickly and easily in the microwave!

2 The ganache can be used warm once it has thickened slightly and is of a pouring consistency, or it can be left to cool so that it can be spread with a palette knife. Alternatively, once completely cool it can be whisked to give a lighter texture.

glacé icing

The simplest of all icings. Make it just before it's needed, as it doesn't keep well.

you will need

- ♡ 300g/10½oz icing (confectioners') sugar
- ♡ 2–4tbsp/30–60ml of water

1 Sieve the icing sugar into a bowl.
2 Gradually beat in the water a little at a time to give a thick, smooth glossy icing.

royal icing

Use royal icing for stencil work and to pipe fine detail.

you will need

- ♡ 1 egg white
- ♡ 250g/9oz icing (confectioners') sugar, sieved

1 Put the egg white in a bowl and lightly beat to break it down.
2 Gradually beat in the icing sugar until the icing is glossy and forms soft peaks.
3 Royal icing can be made in advance and stored, but mustn't be allowed to dry out. Store in the refrigerator in an airtight container and discard any crusted areas before using. If it is too stiff after storage it can be re-beaten to soften it up.

sugarpaste (rolled fondant)

Sugarpaste is a sweet, thick, opaque paste that is soft, pliable, easily coloured and extremely versatile. Ready-made sugarpaste can be bought from supermarkets and cake-decorating suppliers, and is available in the whole colour spectrum. It is also easy and inexpensive to make your own.

you will need (makes 1kg/2¼lb)

- ♡ 4tbsp/60ml cold water
- ♡ 4tsp/20ml/1 sachet powdered gelatine
- ♡ 125ml/4fl oz liquid glucose
- ♡ 15ml/1 tbsp glycerine
- ♡ 1kg/2¼lb icing (confectioners') sugar, sieved, plus extra for dusting

1 Place the water in a small bowl, sprinkle over the gelatine and soak until spongy.

2 Stand the bowl over a pan of hot, but not boiling, water and stir until the gelatine is dissolved. Add the glucose and glycerine, stirring until well blended and runny.

3 Put the icing sugar in a large bowl. Make a well in the centre and slowly pour in the liquid ingredients, stirring constantly. Mix well.

4 Turn out on to a surface dusted with icing sugar and knead until smooth, sprinkling with extra icing sugar if the paste becomes too sticky. The paste can be used immediately or tightly wrapped and stored in a plastic bag until required.

modelling paste

This versatile paste keeps its shape well and dries harder than sugarpaste, but is still edible. It is used throughout the book for adding detail. Although there are commercial pastes available, it is easy and a lot cheaper to make your own.

you will need
(makes 225g/8oz)

♡ 225g/8oz sugarpaste (rolled fondant)

♡ 5ml/1 tsp gum tragacanth (a natural gum available from cake-decorating suppliers)

1 Make a well in the sugarpaste and knead in the gum tragacanth.

2 Wrap in a plastic bag and allow the gum to work before use. You will begin to feel a difference in the paste after an hour or so, but it is best left overnight.

3 The modelling paste should be firm but pliable, with a slight elastic texture. Kneading the modelling paste makes it warm and easy to work with.

modelling paste tips
- If time is short use CMC instead of gum tragacanth; this is a synthetic product but it works almost straight away.
- Placing your modelling paste in a microwave for a few seconds is an excellent way of warming it for use.
- If your paste is crumbly or too hard to work, add a touch of white vegetable fat (shortening) and a little boiled water, and knead until softened.
- If you are making coloured modelling paste, add the colour before the gum has taken effect.

colouring sugarpaste & modelling paste

Brightly coloured sugarpaste (rolled fondant) and modelling paste in all kinds of colours are now available commercially. However, if you can't find the exact colour you're searching for, or if only a small amount of a colour is required, it is often best to colour your own paste or adjust the colour of a commercial one.

Depending on the amount of paste you wish to colour and the depth of colour required, place a little paste colour, not liquid colour, on the end of a cocktail stick (toothpick) or a larger amount on the end of a palette knife. Add the colour to the paste and knead in thoroughly, adding more until the desired result is achieved. Be careful with pale colours, as only a little colour is needed. Deep colours, on the other hand, require plenty and will become quite sticky. To overcome this, add a pinch of gum tragacanth and leave for an hour or two: the gum will make the paste firmer and easier to handle.

Coloured paste will dry slightly darker than it appears when wet.

pastillage

This is an extremely useful paste because, unlike modelling paste, it sets extremely hard. It is not affected by moisture the way other pastes are, and it is used in this book to make coils, swirls and other decorations that are inserted into the cupcakes. Beware, however – the paste crusts quickly and is brittle once dry. You can buy it in a powdered form, to which you add water, but it is easy to make yourself.

you will need (makes 350g/12oz)

- ♡ 1 egg white
- ♡ 300g/11oz icing (confectioners') sugar, sifted
- ♡ 10ml/2 tsp gum tragacanth

1 Put the egg white into a large mixing bowl.

2 Gradually add enough icing sugar until the mixture combines together into a ball.

3 Mix in the gum tragacanth, and then turn the paste out on to a work board or work surface and knead the pastillage well.

4 Incorporate the remaining icing sugar into the remainder of the pastillage to give a stiff paste.

5 Store pastillage in a polythene bag placed in an airtight container in a refrigerator. Use within one month.

sugar syrup

- ♡ 250ml water
- ♡ 250g caster sugar

In a medium saucepan combine sugar and water. Bring to the boil, stirring, until sugar has dissolved (Note: Do not allow to boil for too long or the syrup will be too thick.) Allow to cool.

Replace white sugar with Demerara sugar (a raw sugar) to give a richer flavour. Simple syrup can also be infused with flavours to add a unique twist e.g. vanilla beans, cardamom, root ginger

flowerpaste (petal/gum paste)

Available commercially from sugarcraft suppliers, flowerpaste can be bought in white and a range of colours. There are many varieties available so try a few to see which you prefer. Alternatively, it is possible to make your own, but it is a time-consuming process and you will need a heavy-duty mixer.

you will need
(makes 500g/1lb 2oz)

- ♡ 500g/1lb 2oz icing (confectioners') sugar
- ♡ 15ml/1 tbsp gum tragacanth
- ♡ 25ml/1½ tbsp cold water
- ♡ 10ml/2 tsp powdered gelatine
- ♡ 10ml/2 tsp liquid glucose
- ♡ 15ml/1 tbsp white vegetable fat (shortening)
- ♡ 1 medium egg white

1 Sieve the icing sugar and gum tragacanth into the greased mixing bowl of a heavy-duty mixer (the grease eases the strain on the machine).

2 Place the water in a small bowl, sprinkle over the gelatine and soak until spongy. Stand the bowl over a pan of hot but not boiling water and stir until the gelatine is dissolved. Add the glucose and white fat to the gelatine and continue heating until all the ingredients are melted and mixed.

3 Add the glucose mixture and egg white to the icing sugar. Beat the mixture very slowly until mixed – at this stage it will be a beige colour – then increase the speed to maximum until the paste becomes white and stringy.

4 Grease your hands and remove the paste from the bowl. Pull and stretch the paste several times, and then knead together. Place in a plastic bag and store in an airtight container. Leave the paste to mature for at least 12 hours.

using flowerpaste
Flowerpaste dries quickly, so cut off only as much as you need and reseal the remainder. Work it well with your fingers – it should 'click' between your fingers when it is ready to use. If it is too hard and crumbly add a little egg white and white vegetable fat – the fat slows down the drying process and the egg white makes it more pliable.

sugar glue

Although commercially available, sugar glue is quick and easy to make at home.

1 Break up pieces of sugarpaste into a small container and cover with a little boiling water.
2 Stir until dissolved.
3 This produces a thick glue, which can be easily thinned by adding some more cooled boiled water.

white vegetable fat

This is a solid white vegetable fat (shortening) that is often known by a brand name. The different products are more-or-less interchangeable in cake making. See below for your relevant brand.

UK: Trex or White Flora
South Africa: Holsum
Australia: Copha
USA: Crisco

gum glue

Clear gum glue is available commercially (often known as edible glue) but it is very easy and much cheaper to make it yourself. The basic ingredients are 1 part CMC to 20 parts warm water, which translates into ¼ tsp (1ml) CMC to 2 tbsp (30ml) warm water.

1 Place the CMC into a small container with a lid, add the warm water and shake well.
2 Leave in refrigerator overnight to thicken. In the morning you will have a thick clear glue that can be used to stick your sugar work together.

covering techniques

Once your cupcakes have cooled it is decoration time. How you choose to decorate is largely a matter of taste and personal preference, but time and quantity are also factors. If you are decorating 150 cupcakes for a wedding, adding an intricate design to each is totally impractical. If you wish to treat your best friend to a few special cakes then it is highly appropriate!

preparing the cupcakes

It's worth doing a little preparation before covering your cupcakes. Not all cupcakes come out of the oven perfect — some may need a little trimming with a sharp knife, while others benefit from a little building up with an appropriate icing. Check each of your cupcakes to ensure that the decoration is going to sit just as you want it to, and remedy any that aren't quite right.

buttercream

Beautiful swirls of light and fluffy buttercream are what many strive for, but they are not as simple as they look and there are other options to try!

Try experimenting with different piping tips as you will achieve different effects with quite similar looking tips.

buttercream swirls

1 Place the tip into a large piping bag, then half fill the bag with buttercream. Twist the top of the bag to seal.

2 Holding the bag vertically, start at the centre of the cupcake. Apply pressure to the bag, then move the tip to the edge of the cake and go around the centre in an anti-clockwise direction.

piping tips

to pipe a rose: release the pressure and remove the piping bag when you have completed the circle.

to pipe a swirl: once you have completed the circle, continue piping by adding one or two smaller circles of buttercream on top of the first.

buttercream peaks and domes

1 Hold the bag vertically slightly above the centre of the cupcake.
2 Keeping the bag still, apply pressure to the bag and allow the icing to spread towards the edge of the cupcake.
3 Once it has spread as far as you wish, start to slowly lift the bag while maintaining an even pressure.
4 Release the pressure and remove the bag.

fluffy buttercream

1 Place a dollop of icing in the centre of a cupcake.
2 Using a palette knife spread the icing towards the edges.
3 For a smooth look run the knife across the top; for a fluffier look lightly run the blade around on top of the icing then lift off.

sugarpaste

Using sugarpaste is a very contemporary way of decorating cupcakes.

1 The sugarpaste will need a little help to secure it to the cupcakes, so brush the cakes with an appropriate complementary flavour of syrup or alcohol, or add a thin layer of buttercream or ganache. This also adds flavour and interest to the cake.

2 Knead the sugarpaste until warm and pliable. Roll out on a surface lightly smeared with white vegetable fat (shortening), rather than icing sugar. Roll the paste to a depth of 5mm/³⁄₁₆in. It is a good idea to use spacers for this, as they ensure an even thickness.

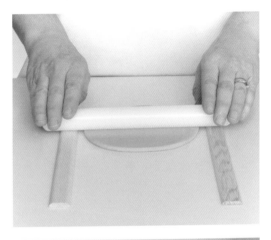

3 Cut out circles of sugarpaste using an appropriately sized cutter. The size of the circle required will be dependant on the cupcake pan and case used, and the amount the cakes have domed.

4 Using a palette knife, carefully lift the paste circles onto each cupcake. Use the palm of your hand to shape the paste to the cupcake, easing the fullness in if necessary.

decorating techniques

stencils

If you have to decorate a large number of cupcakes in a short space of time, then stencilling is always going to be a good choice. You can achieve some impressive results very quickly, but it is always worth trying out the technique before using it on your highly prized cupcakes – practise makes perfect!

edible lustre dust

1 Place your choice of stencil onto the sugarpaste.

2 Roll over the stencil lightly with a rolling pin.

3 Smear white vegetable fat over the pattern then dust the stencil with lustre dust using a soft brush. Carefully remove the stencil.

4 Cut out the pattern using an appropriate circle cutter and attach to the cupcake.

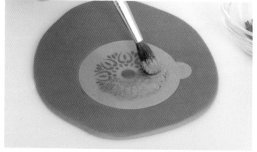

royal icing

1 Adjust the consistency of the icing, if necessary. You need to have the icing fairly thick but still spreadable, so add more icing sugar or water as appropriate.

2 Place the stencil onto rolled out sugarpaste and carefully spread the royal icing over the stencil, removing any excess icing.

3 Once the icing is of an even thickness and you can see the outline of the pattern, gently remove the stencil taking care not to smudge the icing.

4 Immediately cut out the stencilled pattern using an appropriate circle cutter, and place it on top of a cake using a palette knife.

5 Allow the royal icing to dry (this only takes a few minutes) then, with your finger ease in any fullness in the sugarpaste. Allowing the royal icing to dry prevents it being smudged.

moulds

Moulds are an excellent way of creating details to add to your cupcakes quickly and effectively. There are literally thousands of different food grade silicone moulds available, so make time to look around to find ones that you like, and that are a suitable size for the designs you are planning.

Modelling paste is ideal for moulds because it is firmer than straight sugarpaste and therefore easier to use. For small simple moulds, knead the modelling paste, push it firmly into the mould and remove the excess with a palette knife so that the back of the mould is flat. To remove the paste, twist the mould slightly, turn over and flex. For larger or intricate moulds it is easier to add the paste into the mould in sections, pressing down firmly after each addition.

tips on using moulds:

♡ If you are not getting enough detail, check that you are pressing in firmly and your paste is not too stiff.

♡ To introduce various colours into the mould (see p. 66) place the first colour into the mould and press, remove paste from areas you wish to be another colour, then add the next colour and so on until the mould is full.

♡ If you are finding that your moulded shape distorts when it comes out of a particular mould, put the mould in a freezer for 10 minutes or so, before releasing the paste.

cutters

There is a whole host of specialist sugarcraft cutters available, and which you choose will depend on your preferences and the shapes that you are trying to create.

cutting out shapes

Cut outs are very simple to create – just use thinly-rolled modelling paste and your choice of cutters, and then one of the following techniques:

simple shapes

1 Press down onto your paste with the cutter, move the cutter fractionally from side to side (i.e. give it a wiggle) to give a cleaner cut.

2 Remove the excess paste, and ideally leave your paste on your work board for a minute or two before lifting it with a palette knife.

intricate shapes

1 To get a clean cut, rather than pressing a cutter into the rolled out paste, place the paste over the cutter and roll over with a rolling pin.

2 Run your finger over the edges of the cutter, then turn the cutter over and carefully press out the paste using a soft paintbrush.

plastic or metal?

Plastic cutters are usually manufactured in large quantities, and so tend to be available in the basic shapes and sizes that most cake decorators require e.g. hearts and basic flower shapes. They have the advantage that they do not become misshapen with use, however they have to be stored carefully as their cutting edges can become damaged by other tools and cutters. The quality of cutting edges also varies, and they are often not as sharp as fine metal equivalents.

Metal cutters come in an array of designs. Quality varies, so buy the best you can afford. Stainless steel is always preferable to tin plate as it does not rust. You will find that metal cutters come in a range of metal gauges; thinner gauges give a sharper cutting edge but become misshapen more readily, while thicker gauges are more robust but tend not cut as well.

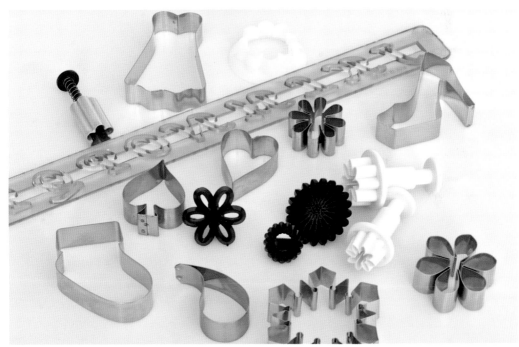

sugar shapers

This tool, which comes with 16 different disc shapes, is a favourite with many sugarcrafters. The secret to using it successfully is to use the correct paste and to make the paste soft enough. To make tassels use modelling paste, and to make twirls and swirls use pastillage. The uses of this amazing tool are only limited by your imagination, so don't be afraid to experiment!

there are two ways to make the paste soft enough:

1 Knead a little white fat into a small ball of paste to stop the paste getting sticky.

2 Dunk the paste into a small container of water and knead.

3 Continue adding firstly white vegetable fat, and then water, until the paste has the consistency of chewed chewing gum – i.e. it is very soft and stretchy, a lot softer than you probably would have thought!

4 Roll the paste into a sausage and insert into the barrel of the sugar shaper.

or

1 Knead a little white fat into a ball of paste.

2 Roll the paste into a sausage and insert into the barrel of the sugar shaper.

3 Place just the filled barrel into a microwave and heat for 10 seconds on the highest setting.

4 Re-assemble the shaper using your chosen disc.

then

5 Push the plunger down to remove any air from the barrel, and hold the tool in your hand with your fingers on the red handle.

6 Pump the handle a few times to increase the pressure in the barrel – you should then find that the softened paste starts to appear.

7 If nothing happens, either you need to build up more pressure by more pumping, or your paste is still too hard.

8 If the paste is too hard, the best thing to do, is to remove the paste and soften it some more, rather than struggling with paste that is too hard!

9 When the paste comes out easily, simply pump when necessary to squeeze out more paste.

twirls

you will need

- ♡ red pastillage
- ♡ sugar shaper
- ♡ no. 42 small star piping tube (PME)
- ♡ edible red dusting powder
- ♡ confectioners' glaze

1 Soften some red pastillage by adding a little white fat and water. Place this together with the small star piping tube into the sugar shaper. Squeeze out a length of paste and wrap around a barbecue skewer or similar to dry.

2 Once completely dry, mix the edible dusting powder with the confectioners glaze and paint over the twirl to brighten the colour and add shine.

flowers

Having a flower on top of your cupcake really completes the design and adds an element of finesse and class. Flowers can be made in a variety of styles and colours, and can be made as quickly as it takes to roll and cut your paste, or as long as you want to style the petals on your intricate rose. A simple change in colour, or layering your flowers on top of each other adds another dimension to your design. Experiment with your colours, cutters and layering and have some fun!

funky flowers (p. 68)

you will need

♡ modelling paste: purple, pink and white

♡ flower cutters:

　large flat floral (LC)

　flat floral collection set 2 (LC)

♡ curved containers in which to dry the flowers

♡ sugar glue

1 Separately roll out the modelling pastes and cut three flowers of different sizes, for each cupcake. Place the flowers singly inside curved containers to dry.

2 Once dry, stack the shapes using a little sugar glue and top with a ball of paste.

daisies (p. 64)

you will need

♡ modelling paste: white, deep pink, light pink, yellow and green

♡ flower moulds:

mini Misc Flower Set FL107 (FI)

small Flower Set FL127 (FI)

blossom plunger cutters (PME)

daisy marguerite cutter (PME)

cutter flowers

1 Thinly roll out the white and deep pink modelling paste and cut a number of white blossoms and two daisy marguerites for each cupcake. Stick one daisy on top of another, positioning the top flower so the petals of the one below are visible. For the centres of the flowers add small balls of green paste to the daisies and light pink paste to the blossoms.

moulded flowers

1 Place yellow modelling paste into the centre of the daisy mould, removing any excess. Fill up the mould with light pink modelling paste and then remove the flower. Dust the edges of the flower with rose dust colour and the centre with lime green.

2 Place white modelling paste into the centre of a small flower mould, removing any excess. Fill up the mould with dark pink modelling paste and remove the flower.

retro flowers (p. 74)

you will need

- ♡ modelling paste: red, white, dark, mid and light blue

- ♡ sugar glue

- ♡ cutters, a selection:

    heart cutter

    paisley for leaves (LC)

    fantasy flowers (PC)

    flat floral sets 1 & 2 (LC)

    daisy centre stamp (JEM)

    daisy marguerite set (PME)

    blossom plunger cutters (PME)

- ♡ piping tube PME no. 4, 32R

1 Thinly roll out each of the modelling pastes and cut out a selection of flowers using the suggested cutters and piping tube. Remove sections from some of the petals using the No 32R PME piping tube.

2 Stack the different flowers in layers of contrasting colours.

3 To create textured centres, roll small balls of paste and press them into the daisy centre stamp. Attach to the flowers as desired.

4 Place some flowers flat on a foam pad to dry and others in small cupped containers such as an egg trays or foil cups.

roses (p. 80)

you will need

♡ rose petal cutters (FMM)

♡ red modelling paste

♡ ball tool

♡ foam pad

1 Roll a small cone of red paste, the same length as the width of the smallest petal cutter.
2 Thinly roll out some red paste and cut out 6 of the smallest and 5 of the second smallest rose petals.
3 Place the petals on a foam pad and run a ball tool round the edge of each petal to soften and frill slightly.

4 Using the smallest petals, wrap one tightly around the tip of the paste cone to create a spiral. Take two petals and wrap these around the cone making sure they stay open at the top. Then take the three remaining small petals and arrange these petals around the cone so they overlap each other, but remain open.

5 To create a fuller rose, add the five larger petals, overlapping them around the centre of the rose. Pinch the outside edges of each of these petals together into a 'V' to help the petals fold back into their characteristic shape.

full bloom flowers (p. 78)

you will need

♡ modelling paste: white and lilac

♡ blossom and daisy micro flowers (LC)

1 Thinly roll out the lilac modelling paste and cut out a selection of micro flowers. Place the flowers on the foam pad and with a ball tool, thin and cup the petals by stroking the tool from the outside of the flower towards the centre of each petal.
2 To make the daisies fuller stick one daisy inside another.

violas (p. 98)

you will need

small violas:

♡ modelling paste: orange, yellow, white and purple

♡ viola mould (FI - small flower set)

♡ dresen tool

large viola:

♡ viola cutters (LC)

♡ green, white and purple flower paste (recipe on p. 36)

♡ ball tool

♡ petal veiner, e.g. tea rose (GI)

♡ leaf veiner, e.g. tea rose leaf (GI)

♡ foam pad

♡ sugar glue

♡ paste colours to paint the viola

♡ dust colours

♡ dusting and fine paintbrushes

♡ clear spirit, e.g. gin or vodka

small violas

1 Roll a small ball of yellow modelling paste and place in the centre of the viola mould.
2 Place white paste into the three lower petals of the mould, using a Dresden tool to help ease the

paste into shape. Add purple paste to the top two petals of the mould.

3 Cut away any excess paste and release the flower from the mould. Leave to dry. Repeat using other colour combinations.

life-size flower calyx

1 Make a small cone of green paste. Pinch the base to form the thin brim of a 'Mexican hat' and cut out using the calyx cutter. Insert a paintbrush into the centre of the calyx to create the flower throat.

life-size viola flower

1 Thinly roll out the white and purple flower pastes. The paste should almost be transparent, so you can see your work board through it.

2 Cut out the petals, two purple and three white,

turn them over and place on a foam pad. Take the ball tool and stroke around the edges of each petal by pressing the tool half on the petal and half on the pad to soften the cut edge.

3 Place one petal at a time onto a double sided veiner and press firmly.

4 Arrange the petals into the throat of the calyx using sugar glue to stick in place. Leave to dry, using pieces of paper towel to hold the petals in position whilst they dry.

5 Once dry, dust the petals as appropriate. Dilute some of the dust in clear spirit and using a fine paintbrush add markings to the petals as desired.

life-size viola leaf

1 Cut out a leaf from thinly rolled green flower paste. Soften the edges with a ball tool and vein in a double sided veiner.

storage

Once the cakes have cooled, store them in an airtight container at room temperature until you are ready to decorate them. Decorate your cakes as close as possible to when they are going to be eaten, to help prevent the cakes drying out. If this is not possible then use foil or high quality greaseproof cases, and cover the whole of the top of the cake to help seal in the moisture.

transport

Cardboard cupcake boxes are the best way to transport your precious cupcakes. They are simply cardboard boxes with an insert that prevents the cakes from sliding around. You can even stack the boxes so that the cupcakes are easy to carry. Boxes are available for the different case sizes, and range in volume from single hole boxes to at least 24 holes.

presentation and display

How you choose to present your cupcakes will depend very much on the occasion, but here are some ideas:

cupcake wrappers

A simple and easy way to jazz up cupcakes, these wrappers are made from paper and just slot around the case of your cupcake – ideal when time is short.

simple party plate

Placing cupcakes on a stylish plate makes any afternoon tea party feel really indulgent.

clear plastic box

Ideal when you want to give a cupcake to a special friend as a gift, or when you wish to give cupcakes away as a going home present for your guests.

cupcake stands

Ideal for when you have a lot of cupcakes to display – these are very popular, especially for weddings. They are available in an increasing number of styles and are usually manufactured from acrylic, plastic or wire. Alternatively, you can make your own using, for example, decorated cake boards and separators, such as cake dummies.

celebrate

vintage chic

Stylish and classic yet contemporary and à la mode, these cameo cupcakes are sure to impress.

you will need

- ♡ cupcakes baked in orange foil cases
- ♡ buttercream or ganache
- ♡ modelling paste: white, orange, golden brown and cream
- ♡ cameo mould (FI – MN221)
- ♡ white vegetable fat
- ♡ sugar shaper
- ♡ sugar glue
- ♡ golden brown royal icing
- ♡ piping bag and tubes no. 1 and 2 (PME)

- ♡ edible gold lustre dust (SK)
- ♡ clear spirit (gin or vodka)
- ♡ 1.5mm/¹⁄₁₆in narrow spacers

Use paper towel to support the loops of the bow while the paste dries.

for the cameo

1 Knead the white modelling paste to warm, then place small sections at a time into the mould to cover the lady but not the background. Use a Dresden tool to encourage the paste into place, removing any excess.

2 Roughly knead some white paste into the orange to create marbled paste, and fill the mould. Carefully remove the paste from the mould and repeat.

3 Warm and soften some golden brown modelling paste by adding a little white vegetable fat and water. Place in the sugar shaper together with the small round disc. Paint sugar glue around the edge of the cameos then squeeze out lengths of paste from the sugar shaper and place around the cameos to form a frame, cutting to fit.

4 Place the cameos onto waxed paper or acetate, then place royal icing into a reusable piping tube fitted with a coupler. Pipe large dots using the no. 2 tube around the outside of the cameo. Once these have dried pipe small dots between the large ones using the no. 1 tube.

5 Once dry, paint over the golden brown paste with edible gold lustre dust mixed with clear spirit.

decorating the cupcakes

6 Add a layer of buttercream or ganache to the cakes.

7 Knead the cream modelling paste to warm and roll out between the spacers. Cut the paste into 4cm (1½in) wide strips.

8 Cut two 12.5cm (5in) lengths. Fold each length in half and gather both ends together to make a bow. Arrange both loops on top of a cupcake.

9 Cut two 10cm (4in) lengths of the cream paste. Cut one end of each at an angle and gather the other for use as the tails. Position on the cake. Cut a short length, pleat it and then tuck around the centre of the bow, to neaten.

10 Attach the prepared cameo to the bow, using royal icing to keep it in place.

back to basics ganache p. 30 ... modelling paste p. 33 ... royal icing p. 31 ...

afternoon tea

These cupcakes are quick and easy to make, so are ideal if you have to make large quantities. Try experimenting with the design by using different cases and topping with a complementary colour to change the look.

you will need

- ♡ cupcakes baked in Swedish violet paper cases
- ♡ buttercream of your choice
- ♡ piping bag, coupler and tubes:
  petal (57R PME),
  round (4 PME),
- ♡ purple sugarpaste

1 Place the coupler into a large piping bag and attach the petal tube, then half fill with buttercream.

2 Starting at the centre of a cupcake, hold the bag so that the thick section of the tube is pointing inwards and the thin section outwards. Start squeezing the bag and draw it out towards the side of the cake and then back into the centre.

3 Repeat, using even pressure for each petal and turning the cupcake in your hand as you pipe.

4 Add a second layer, making the petals shorter.

5 Once you have piped all your cupcakes, roll marbled sized balls of purple sugarpaste and place into the centre of your flowers.

6 Change the tube in the coupler and pipe a circle of small dots around the centre of the flower to complete.

back to basics buttercream p. 28 ... sugarpaste p. 32 ...

zen garden

The Chinese symbol for happiness, which adorns the top of this elegant cupcake, also means 'blessing' or 'good fortune'.

you will need

- ♡ cupcakes baked in black paper cases
- ♡ ganache or buttercream
- ♡ 5mm (³⁄₁₆in) spacers
- ♡ pastillage: red
- ♡ modelling paste: white, dark pink, light pink, yellow and green
- ♡ sugar shaper
- ♡ chinese happiness character cutter (LC)
- ♡ foam pad
- ♡ daisies (x 2 per cake) and white blossom flowers (x 2 per cake)
- ♡ leaves
- ♡ sugar glue

If the paste does not come out of the sugar shaper easily it means that the paste is still too hard. Remove and re-soften.

1 Thinly roll out the pastillage and cut out the happiness characters. Using a palette knife, lift them onto the foam pad to dry.

2 Add a thin layer of buttercream or ganache to the cupcakes.

3 Soften some of the light pink modelling paste and place in the sugar shaper together with the small mesh disc. Squeeze out approximately 8cm (3in) of paste. Place in a curve on top of a cupcake to form the first section of the tassel. Squeeze out more lengths and build up the height.

4 Take a shorter section and wrap around the top of the tassel as the binding. Change the disc in the sugar shaper to the large rope and squeeze out a length. Attach this to the top of the tassel, and coil it around inside the curve to give height to the centre of the cupcake.

5 Insert the pastillage characters into the soft paste of the tassels, securing with sugar glue.

6 Add leaves and flowers, securing with sugar glue.

back to basics ganache p. 30 ... buttercream p. 28 ... pastillage p. 35 ... modelling paste p. 33 ... sugar glue p. 37 ... flowers p. 50 ... Leaves p. 55 ...

card trick

These card deck-themed cupcakes are guaranteed to be trumps with anyone. They are the ideal cake to make with children for Father's Day, or perhaps for a grandpa's birthday.

you will need

- cupcakes baked in red foil cases
- complementary flavour of syrup, alcohol, buttercream or ganache
- sugarpaste: white
- 5mm (³⁄₁₆in) spacers
- cutters:
    circle to fit the top of your cupcakes, card suit cutters (LC)
- playing card embosser (PC)
- modelling paste: black, purple, red and gold
- micro embossers (HP)
- edible gold lustre dust
- clear spirit (gin or vodka)
- black paste colour

1 Brush the cakes with the syrup or alcohol, or add a thin layer of buttercream or ganache to help the sugarpaste stick to the cupcake.

2 Roll out the white sugarpaste between the spacers, and cut out circles using the cutter.

3 Using a palette knife, lift a paste circle carefully onto each cupcake, easing the fullness in if necessary. Run your finger around the edge of each circle to smooth the sugarpaste and to give a rounded appearance.

4 Separately, thinly roll out the red and black modelling pastes. Cut out hearts and diamonds from the red paste, and clubs and spades from the black using the cutters. Attach to the cakes.

5 For the playing card cakes, emboss rolled out white sugarpaste with the jack of clubs embosser. Using the same circle cutter as before, cut circles from the embossed design. Repeat step 3.

6 Thinly roll out the coloured modelling pastes and

emboss each with the card embosser. Cut around the embossed sections using a craft knife and attach to the cakes as desired to create the jack.

7 Emboss some of the jack's robes with the micro embossers to add more detail, and then paint over the gold paste with lustre dust mixed with clear spirit.

8 Dilute the black paste colour with clear spirit. With a fine paintbrush, allow the colour to run into the embossed areas of the face and the 'J'.

back to basics ganache p. 30 ... sugarpaste p. 32 ... buttercream p. 28 ... modelling paste p. 33 ...

flower power

These pretty little cupcakes are the perfect addition for any celebration. Easy to make yet impressive and elegant, they are sure to bring a touch of class to a special day.

you will need

- ♡ cupcakes baked in spotty purple paper cases
- ♡ complementary flavour of syrup, alcohol, buttercream or ganache
- ♡ sugarpaste: pink
- ♡ 5mm (³⁄₁₆in) spacers
- ♡ circle cutter to fit the top of your cupcakes
- ♡ stencil (DS – Winterthur Hearts)
- ♡ royal icing
- ♡ modelling paste: purple and pink
- ♡ white flowers

- ♡ curved containers in which to dry the flowers
- ♡ sugar glue

1 Brush the cakes with the syrup or alcohol, or add a thin layer of buttercream or ganache to help the sugarpaste stick to the cakes.

2 Knead the sugarpaste until warm, then roll out between the spacers.

3 Cut circles to fit the top of the cupcakes, but leave on your work surface.

4 Adjust the consistency of the royal icing, if necessary – see p. 43.

5 Place the stencil onto one of the sugarpaste circles and carefully spread the royal icing over the stencil.

6 Once the icing is of an even thickness, remove the stencil taking care not to smudge the pattern.

7 Using a palette knife, lift the paste circle carefully onto each cupcake, easing in the fullness. of the paste by gently pressing around the edge of the circle.

8 Add the flowers to the cupcakes, using a little sugar glue or royal icing to help them stay in place.

Lift the paste circles onto the cupcake before the royal icing dries and becomes brittle.

back to basics ganache p. 30 ... buttercream p. 28 ... modelling paste p. 33 ... sugarpaste p. 32 ... royal icing p. 31 ... sugar glue p. 37 ... flowers p. 50 ...

wedding

rosy swirls

This attractive rose design is perfect for the big day, especially if the frosting is coloured to match the bride's theme. They are quick and easy to make – ideal if large quantities are required.

you will need

- ♡ cupcakes baked in brown metallic high tea paper cases
- ♡ buttercream of your choice
- ♡ piping bag and large star piping tip
- ♡ pink food colouring

Hold the star tip above the cake surface and let the icing fall into place. You could also try experimenting with other star tips for slightly different effects.

1 Colour a portion of buttercream with the pink food colouring, then colour a small amount deep pink.

2 Place the large star tube into a large piping bag. Put the pink buttercream in one side of your piping bag, a little deep pink in the centre, and then fill the other side of the bag with the uncoloured buttercream – this will give you a piped marbled effect.

3 Holding the bag vertically, start piping at the centre of the cupcake. Apply pressure to the bag, then move the tip to the edge of the cake and go around the centre in a clockwise direction.

4 Release the pressure and remove the piping bag when you have completed the circle.

back to basics buttercream p. 28 ...

lovebird

Vintage is the height of fashion, so why not accessorize your wedding party with these elegant and stylish cakes?

you will need

- ♡ cupcakes baked in blue paper cases
- ♡ buttercream of your choice
- ♡ piping bag
- ♡ pastillage: red
- ♡ modelling paste: red, white, dark, mid and light blue
- ♡ sugar glue
- ♡ superwhite dust
- ♡ cutters: heart, thin leaf, paisley, flowers
- ♡ glass-headed pin

1 Thinly roll out the pastillage and cut out a selection of hearts. Using a palette knife, lift them onto the foam pad to dry.

2 Place the large star tube into a large piping bag and half fill with buttercream.

3 Pressure pipe onto the cupcakes.

4 Top with a flower and pastillage heart.

for the lovebird

5 Roll a 3cm (1³⁄₁₆in) ball of mid blue modelling paste. Using your finger, roll on one side of the ball to create the neck of the bird. Bend the neck upwards to create the head. Take a glass headed pin and indent either side of the head to create eye sockets. Add a small amount of white and dark blue paste for the eyes, and add a cone of dark blue for the beak.

6 Place the bird's body in the centre of a buttercreamed cupcake.

7 Cut out feathers from thinly rolled modelling paste using the thin leaf cutter from the fantasy flower set or similar. Arrange four feathers in a fan for the tail, then add four in a fan shape for each wing. Roll a tapered sausage of mid blue paste to the top of each wing, then attach in place with sugar glue.

8 Cut out a selection of leaves using the paisley cutters and arrange around the bird. Finally, add the prepared heart and flowers to the cake.

back to basics buttercream p. 28 ... pastillage p. 35 ... flowers p. 50 ... modelling paste p. 33 ... sugar glue p. 37 ...

floral fantasy

The perfect treat for the perfect day, and easily coordinated to your colour and floral theme for the ultimate in style. Place in individual gift boxes to give as favours, or use as part of the place settings.

you will need

- ♡ cupcakes baked in silver foil cases
- ♡ complementary flavour of syrup, alcohol, buttercream or ganache
- ♡ sugarpaste: coral pink
- ♡ 5mm (³⁄₁₆in) spacers
- ♡ circle cutter to fit your cupcakes
- ♡ flower embossers: wild rose, tea rose and daisies (PC)
- ♡ royal icing
- ♡ piping bag and tubes no. 1 and 2 (PME)

1 Brush the cakes with syrup or alcohol, or add a thin layer of buttercream or ganache to help the sugarpaste stick to the cakes.

2 Knead the sugarpaste to warm, then roll it out between the spacers. Take your chosen embossers and emboss the sugarpaste.

3 Cut out circles of paste using a circle cutter, positioning the flowers to one side of each circle. Using a palette knife, lift a paste circle carefully onto each cupcake.

4 Place royal icing in the piping bag and fit the no. 2 tube to the coupler. Start at the back of the flower and pipe over the embossed outline of a petal. Now, using a damp paintbrush, gently stroke the inner edge of the piped outline towards the base of the petal to give a softer, feathered appearance. Repeat for the remaining petals.

5 Change the tube to no. 1 and pipe small dots as patterns, in the centre of each flower. Do this in stages on each flower so that you create a textured centre. Add extra dots as decoration as you choose.

back to basics ganache p. 30 ... sugarpaste p. 32 ... royal icing p. 31 ... buttercream p. 28 ... sugar syrup p. 35 ...

tiered miniature

Imagine a tiered cake stand brimming with these stylish cakes on your big day. Elegant and contemporary, they are sure to go down a treat with your guests and add to the memories of your day.

you will need

- cupcakes baked in purple foil cases
- complementary flavour of syrup, alcohol, buttercream or ganache
- sugarpaste: purple
- 5mm (³⁄₁₆in) spacers
- circle cutter to fit the top of your cupcakes
- five point medallion stencil (DS)
- royal icing
- superwhite dust
- modelling paste: white
- daisies: lilac

- blossom and daisy micro flowers (LC)
- ball tool
- sugar glue
- piping bag and tubes no. 0 & 2 (PME)

1 Brush the cakes with the syrup or alcohol, or add a thin layer of buttercream or ganache to help the sugarpaste stick.

2 Knead the sugarpaste to warm, then roll out between the spacers.

3 Mix the superwhite into the royal icing to whiten it. Adjust the consistency of the icing, if necessary – you need to have the icing fairly thick but still spreadable, so add more icing sugar or water as appropriate.

4 Place the stencil onto the sugarpaste and carefully spread the royal icing over the top. Once the icing is of an even thickness remove the stencil, taking care not to smudge the pattern. Cut out the patterns using an appropriate circle cutter.

5 Using a palette knife, lift a paste circle carefully onto each cupcake, easing the fullness in if necessary. Run your finger around the edge of each circle to smooth the sugarpaste. Repeat for the remaining cupcakes.

6 Roll three sausages of modelling paste to the following widths: 3cm (1 ³⁄₁₆in), 2cm (¾in) & 1cm (³⁄₈in). Take a palette knife and cut the wider two

back to basics ganache p. 30 ... buttercream p. 28 ... flowers p. 50 ...

sausages into 1.2cm (½in) segments, then cut the thinnest sausage into 1cm (⅜in) segments. Re-roll each segment to bring it back to a true circular shape, then stack the segments in descending sizes on top of some of your cupcakes to create the stacked cake.

7 Make your miniature daisies following the instructions for full bloom flowers (see p. 53).

8 Arrange some daisies around the base of the middle tier, allowing a little room between each flower. Add three daisies to the top of each cake.

9 Place royal icing into a reusable piping tube fitted with a coupler, and pipe dots of different sizes, inside each flower, around the base of each tier and onto the stencilled cake, using the piping tubes suggested.

sugarpaste p. 32 ... royal icing p. 31 ... modelling paste p. 33 ... sugar glue p. 37 ...

wedding 79

roses are red

With funky colours for a classic wedding, these cupcakes will create quite an impact when lined up on a tiered stand.

you will need

- ♡ cupcakes baked in high tea metallic black paper cases
- ♡ buttercream of your choice
- ♡ piping bag
- ♡ double-sided feather veiner (GI)
- ♡ large star tip
- ♡ roses
- ♡ twirls

1 Thinly roll out some black modelling paste and place inside the double-sided feather veiner. Squeeze the two sides of the veiner together and remove the excess paste from the edges. Open the veiner and trim the resulting feather with scissors if necessary. Allow the feather to dry (about 30 minutes) over a small cylindrical shape.

2 Place the large star tube into a piping bag and half fill with buttercream. Pressure pipe the buttercream onto your cupcakes in the style of your choice.

3 Top the buttercream with one, or all, of the prepared decorations.

4 If desired, place a cupcake wrapper around a selection of the cakes to complete.

back to basics flowers p. 50 ... twirls p. 49 ... buttercream p. 28 ... modelling paste p. 33 ...

children

birthday bears

These cupcakes are ideal for a special birthday party or teddy bear's picnic. Try varying the design to match a favourite soft toy.

you will need

- cupcakes baked in pink foil cases
- complementary flavour of syrup, buttercream or ganache
- sugarpaste: pink
- 5mm (³⁄₁₆in) spacers
- circle cutter to fit the top of your cupcakes
- heart stencil (DS – holiday cookie tops)
- royal icing: pink
- modelling paste: golden brown, dark pink, pink, brown, white and lime green
- flower cutter/ embosser (FMM – Flowers 1)
- ball tool
- stitching wheel
- sugar glue
- dried spaghetti
- U tool (PME)
- cutting wheel (PME)

1 Brush the cakes with the syrup or alcohol, or add a thin layer of buttercream or ganache to help the sugarpaste stick to the cakes.

2 Knead the sugarpaste to warm, then roll out between the spacers.

3 Place the stencil onto the sugarpaste and carefully spread the royal icing over the stencil.

4 Once the icing is of an even thickness, remove the stencil taking care not to smudge the pattern.

5 Cut out the patterns using an appropriate circle cutter. Using a palette knife, lift a paste circle carefully onto each cupcake, easing the fullness in if necessary. Run your finger around the edge of each circle to smooth the sugarpaste.

7 For the body of the teddy, roll a 3cm (1³⁄₁₆in) ball of golden brown modelling paste then roll into a cone. Run the stitching

Practise your royal icing on a piece of spare sugarpaste first, then you'll know how thickly you wish to apply it.

wheel from the bottom to the top of the cone to form the teddy's centre seam. Place on the cake.

8 For the legs, roll a 1.8cm (¾in) ball of paste and cut in half. Roll each half into a sausage 2.5cm (1in) long. Thin the ankles by rolling the paste between your fingers  and then pinch the ends to form feet. Use the small end of the ball tool to indent the pads of the feet. Fill each indent with a small ball of pink paste. Attach to the body using sugar glue.

9 For the arms, roll two 4cm (1½in) sausages of paste, thin the wrists and add pink sugarpaste pads. Attach to the body with sugar glue.

10 Insert a length of spaghetti through the body to help support the head. Roll a 2.3cm (⅞in) ball of paste and place on top of the spaghetti. Run a stitching wheel over the top of the head, then add a flattened 1cm (⅜in) ball for the muzzle. Use a U tool to create his mouth.

11 For the ears, indent either side of the head with a Dresden tool or the end of a paintbrush. Roll 5mm (³⁄₁₆in) balls of paste, indent each with a ball tool, then pinch one side to create a point. Insert this into the prepared holes to secure.

12 Add eyes and a nose using small balls of brown and white paste.

13 Cut out a flower and leaf and attach to one ear.

14 Finally, create a blanket by thinly rolling out green paste, cutting out a small rectangle and gathering one end. Attach to one paw to complete.

back to basics buttercream p. 28 ... ganache p. 30 ... modelling paste p. 33 ... royal icing p. 31 ... sugar glue p. 37 ...

play time

The perfect solution for today's busy mums – each cupcake is decorated with bright and colourful ball pool balls, while a special cake features the birthday boy or girl. Use coloured sweets in place of the balls if you're really short of time.

you will need

♡ cupcakes baked in orange paper cases

♡ ganache

♡ modelling paste in a variety of bright colours, plus flesh

♡ dried spaghetti

♡ sugar glue

♡ superwhite dust

♡ piping bag and tube no.16 (PME)

♡ strawberry calyx cutter (JEM) or similar

1 Roll 1.5cm (⅝in) balls of modelling paste in your choice of colours.

2 Spread ganache over each cupcake and top with a heap of paste balls.

3 Roll a 1.2cm (½in) x 9cm (3½in) sausage. Indent both ends with a paintbrush. Arrange as the arms in a 'U' shape on top of one pile of balls.

4 For the hands, roll a 1cm (⅜in) ball of modelling paste and cut in half. Take one half and roll into a ball, then pinch half of the ball with one hand and rotate to form a wrist. Flatten the other half to form the child's hand. With a pair of small scissors cut out a small triangle for the thumb. Attach the wrist to the arm, using sugar glue. Repeat for the second hand.

5 Roll a 3cm (1in) ball of flesh-coloured modelling paste then, holding the widest end of the piping tube at 45°, indent a mouth. Use the smaller end of the tube to indent the corners of the mouth.

6 Indent eye sockets with a cocktail stick and then add small balls of black paste for the eyes, and a small ball of flesh paste for the nose.

7 Add a light spot to each eye by mixing a little superwhite dust with water and painting a dot with a fine paintbrush.

8 Attach the head in place, using spaghetti and glue at the base to secure.

9 Thinly roll out some brown modelling paste, cut out a strawberry calyx or similar, and attach to the head as hair.

back to basics ganache p. 30 ... modelling paste p. 33 ... sugar glue p. 37 ...

odd socks

These colourful cupcakes are ideal for a birthday party or christening – or why not take them as presents to a baby shower?

you will need

- ♡ cupcakes baked in pastel-coloured foil cases

- ♡ complementary flavour of syrup, alcohol, buttercream or ganache

- ♡ sugarpaste: white, green and pink

- ♡ 5mm (³⁄₁₆in) spacers

- ♡ fluted circle cutter to fit the top of your cupcakes

- ♡ small sock cutter (LC)

- ♡ piping bag and tube no. 16 (PME)

- ♡ modelling paste: purple, green, white, dark pink, light pink, brown and orange

1 Brush the cakes with the syrup or alcohol, or add a thin layer of buttercream or ganache to help the sugarpaste stick to the cakes.

2 Knead the sugarpaste to warm, then roll it out between the spacers.

3 Cut out fluted circles of sugarpaste with the cutter.

4 Using a palette knife, lift a paste circle carefully onto each cupcake. Use the palm of your hand to shape the paste to the cupcake, easing the fullness in if necessary.

5 Separately, roll out the different colours of modelling paste to a thickness of 1.5mm (⅝in). Cut out socks and a selection of circles using the suggested cutters.

6 Cut away the toe, heel and top of each sock and replace it with one of another colour. Texture the top of each sock with the edge of a palette knife.

7 Cut circles from the centre of each sock and replace with circles of other colours. Rub a finger over the top of each circle to blend the paste.

8 Use a small paintbrush and a little water to help stick the socks to the tops of the cupcakes.

back to basics ganache p. 30 ... buttercream p. 28 ... modelling paste p. 33 ... sugarpaste p. 32 ...

perfect pets

These funky rag toy designs will make a fun and colourful addition to any children's party.

you will need

- cupcakes baked in red paper cases
- complementary flavour of syrup, buttercream or ganache
- sugarpaste: peach
- 5mm (0.2in) spacers
- mini embossers: e.g. set 1, 2,10,11,12 (HP)
- circle cutter to fit the top of your cupcakes
- selection of small shape cutters, e.g. oval, heart paisley (LC), teardrop (LC)
- plunger flower (PME)
- piping bag and tubes no. 18, 17, 16 and 4 (PME)
- modelling paste: green, blue, deep pink, black, white

The dog is made with a heart for his body, an oval for his head and two paisleys for his ears. The cat has a paisley for its body and oval for its head. The rabbit is made from ovals and teardrops.

1 Brush the cakes with the syrup or alcohol, or add a thin layer of buttercream or ganache to help the sugarpaste stick to the cakes.

2 Knead the sugarpaste until warm, then roll it out between the spacers.

3 Take one or more of the small embossers and press repeatedly into the sugarpaste to create a textured pattern on the paste.

4 Cut out circles from the textured sugarpaste using the cutter. With a palette knife, carefully lift a paste circle onto each cupcake.

5 Separately, roll out the different colours of modelling paste to a thickness of 1.5mm (⅛in) and texture some or all with the mini embossers.

6 Cut out a selection of shapes, using the photo as a guide, and use to create your own rag toys.

7 Attach the toys to the top of the cupcakes using a small paintbrush and a little water or sugar glue.

8 Add a flower or two to complete.

back to basics ganache p. 30 ... buttercream p. 28 ... modelling paste p. 33 ... sugarpaste p. 32 ... flowers p. 50 ...

rubber ducky

Surprisingly easy to make and sure to thrill, these cupcakes are ideal for a children's party…or maybe even an adult's?!

you will need

- ♡ cupcakes baked in white paper cases (you want the top of the cakes to be below the edge of the case, so be careful not to overfill)
- ♡ glacé icing
- ♡ modelling paste: yellow, orange and black
- ♡ dried spaghetti
- ♡ sugar glue
- ♡ superwhite dust (SF)

1 Roll a 2.5cm (1½in) ball of yellow modelling paste. Pinch a section of paste to form the tail, and then pinch across the tail to make it more pointed. Shape by stroking the tail up.

2 Next, roll a 1.75cm (1¾in) ball for the head. Insert a small length of spaghetti into the front of the body to support the head, then position the ball on top, using sugar glue at the base to secure.

3 For the wings, roll a 1.5cm (⅝in) ball of paste and cut in half. Take one half and roll into another ball. Pinch half of the ball with one hand and the other half at 90° with the other hand to make a rough wing shape. Use your fingers to refine the shape. Repeat and attach in place with sugar glue.

4 For the eyes, indent eye sockets using a cocktail stick. Roll a small ball of black modelling paste and cut in half. Re-roll each half and insert into the indented sockets.

5 Add a light spot to each eye by mixing a little superwhite dust with water and painting a dot with a fine paintbrush.

6 For the beak, roll a 5mm (³⁄₁₆in) ball of orange modelling paste into a cone. Cut the point of the cone in two with scissors. Pinch each half to shape and then curve slightly. Using the end of a paintbrush, indent a hole for the beak in the head, and secure the beak in place with sugar glue.

7 Roll a small thin sausage of paste, coil it and attach to the top of the duck's head to complete.

8 Make the glacé icing and spoon over the cooled cakes.

9 Position the duck in place.

If your 'water' is too deep and your duck sinks, place a little modelling paste underneath his body to give him a little lift.

back to basics glacé icing p. 31 ... modelling paste p. 33 ... sugar glue p. 37 ...

seasonal

beautiful butterfly

Simple, elegant and beautiful, these cupcakes are the epitome of style. The delicate butterfly perched on top of the luscious buttercream is guaranteed to impress your guests and have them marvelling at your baking prowess.

you will need

- ♡ cupcakes baked in purple paper cases
- ♡ buttercream of your choice
- ♡ piping bag and large star tip
- ♡ purple flowers
- ♡ card for butterfly former
- ♡ monarch butterfly cutter (LC)
- ♡ pastillage

1 Make a former by folding a small piece of card into a 'V' shape, then fold a small section of kitchen paper and place on top of the card.

2 Thinly roll out the pastillage and cut out using the butterfly cutter. Transfer the shape to the former, using a palette knife, and position in the 'V' to dry, so that the wings rest one on either side.

3 Once the butterfly is completely dry (ideally overnight), dilute the orange paste colour in clear spirit and gently paint over the wings of the butterfly in sweeping strokes. Allow to dry.

4 Add some brown paste colour into a small amount of orange modelling paste and roll into a thin sausage. Attach to the butterfly to create a body.

5 Dilute some of the brown paste colour in a small amount of clear spirit and, using a fine paintbrush, paint the brown wing markings onto the butterfly. Allow to dry.

6 Mix the superwhite dust with confectioner's glaze (which stops the brown colour seeping into and spoiling the white). With a fine paintbrush, paint dots of white around the wing tips and on the body, as illustrated.

7 Place the large star tube into a large piping bag and half fill with buttercream. Pressure pipe the buttercream onto your cupcakes in the style of your choice, and top with a flower or butterfly.

back to basics pastillage p. 35 ... flowers p. 50 ... buttercream p. 28 ...

spring violas

Bright, colourful and cheerful, these cupcakes are the essence of spring.

you will need

- ♥ cupcakes baked in purple paper cases
- ♥ buttercream of your choice
- ♥ violas in a variety of colours and sizes
- ♥ pastillage: cream
- ♥ white fat
- ♥ sugar shaper
- ♥ piping bag, coupler and large round piping tube

1 Soften some cream pastillage by adding a little white fat and water. Place this together with the small round disc into the sugar shaper. Squeeze out a length of paste onto a foam pad and arrange in a coil shape. Repeat and leave to dry thoroughly.

2 Place the large round tube into a large piping bag and half fill with buttercream. Pressure pipe the icing onto your cupcakes in the style of your choice.

3 Top the small cupcakes with a moulded flower and the standard cupcakes with a life-size sugar flower and leaf. Finish off by inserting a couple of pastillage coils into the buttercream.

back to basics buttercream p. 28 ... pastillage p. 35 ... flowers p. 57 ... leaf calyx p. 55 ...

falling leaves

These beautiful cupcakes are the ideal accompaniment to an autumnal party or bonfire night. The maple leaves are delicate yet easy to make, and add a real touch of style and class.

you will need

- ♡ cupcakes baked in orange paper cases
- ♡ buttercream of your choice
- ♡ Japanese maple leaf cutters
- ♡ maple leaf veiner (SK)
- ♡ flower paste: golden brown
- ♡ foam pad
- ♡ ball tool
- ♡ edible dusts in autumnal colours (reds, browns and oranges)
- ♡ piping bag, coupler and large round tube

1 Smear white fat over your work board to stop the paste sticking, then very thinly roll out the flower pastes.

2 Cut out a leaf, turn it over and place on a foam pad. Take the ball tool and stroke around the edges of the each petal by pressing the tool half on the petal and half on the pad to soften the cut edge.

3 Place the leaf onto one side of the double veiner, place the other side on top and press firmly. Remove the leaf and place on scrunched-up paper towel in a life like shape to dry. Repeat.

4 Once dry, dust the leaves with a selection of red, brown, yellow and orange dusts. Set the dusts by very carefully passing each leaf through steam from a kettle.

5 Place the large round tube into a large piping bag and half fill with buttercream.

6 Pressure pipe the icing onto your cupcakes in the style of your choice.

7 Top each cupcake with one or more of the leaves.

The flower paste should be rolled so that it is almost transparent. You should be able to see your work board through it.

back to basics modelling paste p. 33 ... buttercream p. 28 ...

snowflakes

A stunning winter alternative to the traditional yule logs and mince pies. Simple yet stylish, these are sure to go down a treat at any Christmas party.

you will need

- ♡ cupcakes baked in white paper cases
- ♡ white royal icing or white frosting of your choice
- ♡ snowflake cutters
- ♡ pastillage
- ♡ superwhite dust
- ♡ 1.5mm (¹⁄₁₆in) spacers
- ♡ selection of small cutters and tubes no. 4,16 and 32R (PME)
- ♡ foam pads
- ♡ piping bag, coupler and large star piping tube

1 Whiten the pastillage by kneading in some superwhite dust. Roll out some of the paste between the narrow spacers, then place it over a snowflake cutter.

2 Roll over the paste with a rolling pin. Run your finger over the edges of the cutter to achieve a clean cut. Turn the cutter over and carefully press out the paste using a soft paintbrush. This gives you your outline shape.

3 Take either small cutters or piping tubes and remove a selection of small shapes radiating out from the centre.

4 Leave on your workboard until the paste has hardened, to prevent the snowflake distorting.

5 Place on a foam pad and dry thoroughly (ideally overnight). An airing cupboard is an ideal place to dry pastillage, as the gentle heat removes all the moisture from the paste.

6 Place the large star tube into a large piping bag and half fill with icing.

7 Pressure pipe the icing onto your cupcakes in the style of your choice and immediately insert a dried snowflake vertically into the soft icing on each cake.

back to basics pastillage p. 35 ... royal icing p. 31 ...

festive firs

No Christmas party should be without these elegant cupcakes. Try different seasonal colour combinations, or present your cakes in a stylish box as the perfect gift.

you will need

- ♥ cupcakes baked in metallic red paper cases
- ♥ complementary flavour of syrup, alcohol, buttercream or ganache
- ♥ sugarpaste: green
- ♥ 5mm (³⁄₁₆in) spacers
- ♥ fluted circle cutter to fit the top of your cupcakes
- ♥ small Christmas tree stencil (DS)
- ♥ royal icing
- ♥ superwhite dust

1 Brush the cakes with syrup or alcohol, or add a thin layer of buttercream or ganache to help the sugarpaste stick.

2 Knead the sugarpaste to warm, then roll out between the spacers.

3 Mix the superwhite into the royal icing to whiten it, and adjust the consistency of the icing – you need to have the icing fairly thick but still spreadable, so be prepared to add more icing sugar or water as necessary.

4 Place the stencil onto the sugarpaste and carefully spread the royal icing over the stencil. Once the icing is of an even thickness, remove the stencil, taking care not to smudge the pattern.

5 Cut out the tree patterns using the fluted circle cutter. Using a palette knife, lift a paste circle carefully onto each cupcake, easing the fullness in if necessary. Run your finger around the edge of each circle to smooth the sugarpaste.

back to basics ganache p. 30 ... buttercream p. 28 ... sugarpaste p. 32 ... royal icing p. 31 ...

designer

animal print

These sublime chocolate cupcakes, complete with personalized animal print decoration are sure to be a wild success.

you will need

- ♡ cupcakes baked in leopard print paper cases
- ♡ complementary flavour buttercream or ganache
- ♡ 3cm (1⅛in) circle cutter
- ♡ script letter cutters (FMM)
- ♡ piping bag and coupler
- ♡ piping tubes no. 18, 16 and 4 (PME)
- ♡ modelling paste: dark brown, mid brown and cream
- ♡ craft knife
- ♡ foam pad

1 Knead each colour of the modelling paste well and roll into thin sausages.

2 Place 4 or 5 sausages of the dark brown paste around a mid brown one, then add further cream sausages around the dark brown ones (you may need a little water to help them stick together). Roll all together to elongate the sausage. Repeat.

3 With a sharp craft knife, cut through the sausages at 2.5cm (1in) intervals. Place the cut sections on top of each other to create parallel bands of colour running through the paste. Squeeze to ensure the sections have stuck together and there are no gaps.

4 Carefully slice across the length of the paste every 3mm (⅛in), then roll over the slices with a rolling pin to thin the paste to 1.5mm (⅟₁₆in).

5 Cut 3cm (1in) circles from the paste, then cut small circles using the piping tubes from the remainder.

6 Finally cut out appropriate letters from the dark brown and cream pastes, and attach first the brown letter and then the cream to the centre of each large disc.

7 Place all onto a foam pad to dry.

8 Spread a layer of buttercream or ganache over the cakes. Take a palette knife and, starting at the edge of the cupcake, make circular strokes over the icing to create a rough circular or spiral pattern – don't worry about being especially neat.

9 Add the dried letter discs to the tops of the cupcakes and the smaller discs in a spiral.

back to basics buttercream p. 28 ... ganache p. 30 ... modelling paste p. 33 ...

a touch of class

The classic colour combinations of purple and bronze bring class and style to these cakes. The stencils are available in a wide range of classic patterns, or why not try some stencil lettering for that personal touch?

you will need...

- ♡ cupcakes baked in fuchsia pink paper cases
- ♡ complementary flavour of syrup, alcohol, buttercream or ganache
- ♡ sugarpaste: purple
- ♡ 5mm (³⁄₁₆in) spacers
- ♡ circle cutter to fit the top of your cupcakes
- ♡ stencils, such as mehndi and rosette (DS)
- ♡ white vegetable fat
- ♡ edible bronze lustre dust (SK)

1 Brush the cakes with syrup or alcohol, or add a thin layer of buttercream or ganache to help the sugarpaste stick to the cakes.

2 Knead the sugarpaste to warm, then roll it out between the spacers. Now place your choice of stencil onto the sugarpaste and roll over the stencil lightly with a rolling pin. Smear white vegetable fat over the pattern, then dust the stencil with lustre dust using a soft brush. Carefully remove the stencil.

3 Cut out the pattern using circle cutter. Using a palette knife, lift a paste circle carefully onto each cupcake, easing the fullness in if necessary. Run your finger around the edge of each circle to smooth the sugarpaste.

back to basics ganache p. 30 ... sugarpaste p. 32 ... buttercream p. 28 ... sugar syrup p. 35 ...

floral elegance

The classic black, pink and red colour combinations on these little cakes make them a stylish and chic treat for any occasion.

you will need

♡ cupcakes baked in Swedish Amaryllis paper cases

♡ complementary flavour of syrup, alcohol, buttercream or ganache

♡ sugarpaste: white

♡ 5mm (³⁄₁₆in) spacers

♡ fantasy flower embossers (PC)

♡ circle cutter to fit the top of your cupcakes

♡ piping tubes no. 16 and 4 (PME)

♡ moulded flowers

♡ paste colour: dark green

Adjust the colour of your flowers to match different cupcake cases.

1 Brush the cakes with the syrup or alcohol, or add a thin layer of buttercream or ganache to help the sugarpaste stick to the cakes.

2 Knead the sugarpaste to warm, then roll it out between the spacers.

3 Cut circles from the sugarpaste using an appropriate cutter, but leave them on your work board.

4 Emboss each circle with the pattern of your choice, using the embossers from the fantasy flower.

5 Thinly roll out the black modelling paste and cut narrow strips using the craft knife, and small circles using the suggested piping tubes and attach as desired to the cupcakes.

6 Attach one large and one small flower to the cupcakes using water or sugar glue.

7 Dilute the green paste colour and paint over the centres of each flower to create depth.

back to basics ganache p. 30 ... buttercream p. 28 ... flowers p. 50 ... modelling paste p. 33 ... sugarpaste p. 32 ...

shopping spree

The height of elegance and style, these cupcakes are perfect for that fashion-conscious girl about town.

you will need

- ♡ cupcakes in your choice of flavour, baked in orchid paper cases
- ♡ complementary flavour of syrup, alcohol, buttercream or ganache
- ♡ sugarpaste: pink
- ♡ 5mm (0.2in) spacers
- ♡ fantasy flower embossers (PC)
- ♡ cutters: circle to fit the top of your cupcakes, small platform stiletto shoe (LC),
- small party dress (LC), small daisy marguerite cutter (PME)
- ♡ mini flower embosser – set 1 (HP)
- ♡ modelling paste: 3 shades of green and 2 shades of pink
- ♡ cutting wheel

1 Brush the cakes with the syrup or alcohol, or add a thin layer of buttercream or ganache to help the sugarpaste stick to the cakes

2 Knead the sugarpaste to warm, then roll it out between the spacers

3 Cut circles from the sugarpaste using an appropriate cutter but leave them on your board.

4 Emboss sections of each circle with embossers from the fantasy flower set to create a textured pattern.

5 With a palette knife, carefully lift the textured paste circles onto the cupcakes.

6 Roll out the deep pink modelling paste to a thickness of 1.5mm (1/16in) and cut out the shoes and dresses.

7 Roll small pea-sized balls of paste, cut each in half and place the two halves under each of the modelling paste dresses to create busts.

8 Emboss the hem of the dresses with the mini flower embosser.

9 Using your little finger, stroke the paste from below the bust to the hem to create folds on each dress, and attach to the cupcakes.

10 Very thinly roll out the green modelling pastes and cut thin strips using a craft knife. Attach these to the dress to make a striped band.

11 Add a double flower using the daisy marguerite cutter plus a small ball of paste for the centre.

12 Using a cutting wheel, remove the heels from the cut out shoes. Cut others from the light pink paste and attach both parts of the shoes to the cupcakes.

13 Emboss the top edge of the shoe and add stripes and a flower as described above to complement the dress.

back to basics buttercream p. 28 ... ganache p. 30 ... modelling paste p. 33 ... sugarpaste p. 32 ...

retro party

Stylish and contemporary, these colourful cakes are guaranteed to bring a burst of happiness and cheer to any party. Co-ordinate the colours to the event or guests for that added touch of sophistication.

you will need...

- ♡ cupcakes baked in lime green spotty paper cases
- ♡ complementary flavour of syrup, alcohol, buttercream or ganache
- ♡ sugarpaste: white and blue
- ♡ 5mm (³⁄₁₆in) spacers
- ♡ set of circle and square cutters (FMM – geometric set)
- ♡ piping bag and tubes no. 18, 16 and 4 (PME)

1 Brush the cakes with a syrup or alcohol, or add a thin layer of buttercream or ganache to help the sugarpaste stick to the cakes.

2 Knead the sugarpaste to warm, then roll it out between the spacers. Cut out one circle for each cake, using a circle cutter.

3 Using a palette knife, lift a paste circle carefully onto each cupcake, easing the fullness in if necessary. Run your finger around the edge of each circle to smooth the sugarpaste and to give it a rounded appearance.

4 Separately, roll out the different colours of modelling paste to a thickness of 1.5mm (¹⁄₁₆in). Cut out a selection of circles and squares of varying designs and sizes, using the suggested cutter set. Use these shapes to decorate the cupcakes.

5 Top each cupcake with a ball of sugarpaste.

Use a small paintbrush and a little water to help stick the shapes in place on each layer

---

back to basics modelling paste p. 33 ... ganache p. 30 ... sugarpaste p. 32 ... buttercream p. 28 ... sugar syrup p. 35 ...

suppliers

UK

Lindy's Cakes Ltd (LC)
Unit 2 Station Approach
Wendover
Bucks
HP22 6BN
Tel: +44 (0)1296 622418
www.lindyscakes.co.uk
Manufacturer of cutters plus online shop for equipment used in Lindy's books

Knightbridge PME Ltd
Chadwell Heath Lane
Romford
Essex
RN6 4NP
Tel: +44 (0)208 590 5959
www.cakedecoration.co.uk
Sugarcraft cutter supplier and UK distributor of Wilton products

M&B Specialised Confectioners Ltd
3a Millmead Estate
Mill Mead road
London
N17 9ND
Tel: +44 (0)208 801 7948
www.mbsc.co.uk
Manufacturers and suppliers of sugarpaste

US

Global Sugar Art
625 Route 3, Unit 3
Plattsburgh, NY 12901
Tel: 518 561 3039
www.globalsugarart.com
Sugarcraft supplier that imports many UK products to the US

First Impressions Molds
P.O. Box 1598
Loxahatchee, FL 33470
Tel: 561 784 7186
www.firstimpressionsmolds.com

Australia

Iced Affair
53 Church Street
Camperdown
NSW 2050
Tel: (02) 9519 3679
www.icedaffair.com.au

Abbreviations used in this book
DS - Designer Stencils
FI – First Impressions
FMM - FMM Sugarcraft
GI – Great impressions
HP - Holly Products
JEM - JEM Cutter
LC - Lindy's Cakes Ltd
PC - Patchwork Cutters
PME - PME Sugarcraft
PO – Paper Orchid
SF – Sugarflair
SK – Squires Kitchen

about the author

Lindy Smith is a talented world-class cake designer, who shares her love of sugarcraft and inspires fellow enthusiasts by writing books and teaching. Lindy is the author of six cake decorating titles for D&C: **Creative Celebration Cakes, Storybook Cakes, Celebrate with a Cake!, Party Animal Cakes, Cakes to Inspire and Desire** and **Bake Me I'm Yours... Cookie.**

Lindy's teaching takes her all around the world, giving her the opportunity to educate and inspire whilst also learning about local traditions and cake decorating issues. She has appeared on television in programmes such as **The Generation Game** and presented a sugarcraft series on **Good Food Live.**

Lindy also heads Lindy's Cakes Ltd, a well established business that runs her online shop, **www.lindyscakes.co.uk**, and cake decorating workshops both in the UK and abroad. To see what Lindy is currently doing, become a fan of Lindy's Cakes on Facebook or follow Lindy on Twitter. For baking advice and a wealth of information visit her blog via the Lindy's Cakes website.

acknowledgments

I would like to thank my team at Lindy's cakes for helping me decide which of all the tasty recipes we sampled I should include in this book – now you can try the recipes out for yourselves girls! I'd also like to thank all my enthusiastic students, customers, Facebook fans and Twitter and blog followers, with out your many and varied comments and questions my books wouldn't be so easy to write!

index